ISBN 978-1-331-50184-8
PIBN 10198727

1 MONTH OF
FREE
READING

at

www.ForgottenBooks.com

By purchasing this book you are eligible for one month membership to ForgottenBooks.com, giving you unlimited access to our entire collection of over 700,000 titles via our web site and mobile apps.

To claim your free month visit:
www.forgottenbooks.com/free198727

English
Français
Deutsche
Italiano
Español
Português

www.forgottenbooks.com

Mythology Photography **Fiction**
Fishing Christianity **Art** Cooking
Essays Buddhism Freemasonry
Medicine **Biology** Music **Ancient**
Egypt Evolution Carpentry Physics
Dance Geology **Mathematics** Fitness
Shakespeare **Folklore** Yoga Marketing
Confidence Immortality Biographies
Poetry **Psychology** Witchcraft
Electronics Chemistry History **Law**
Accounting **Philosophy** Anthropology
Alchemy Drama Quantum Mechanics
Atheism Sexual Health **Ancient History**
Entrepreneurship Languages Sport
Paleontology Needlework Islam
Metaphysics Investment Archaeology
Parenting Statistics Criminology
Motivational

LONDON CHRONICLE

DURING THE REIGNS OF

HENRY THE SEVENTH AND HENRY THE EIGHTH.

EDITED,

FROM THE ORIGINAL MS. IN THE COTTONIAN LIBRARY OF
THE BRITISH MUSEUM,

BY CLARENCE HOPPER.

PRINTED FOR THE CAMDEN SOCIETY.
M.DCCC.LIX.

INTRODUCTION.

THE writer of this Chronicle appears to have been a citizen of London. He duly records under each mayoralty the occurrences of the year, but more especially those events which particularly relate to the City. He notes the progresses of the Royal Family, the arrival of illustrious visitors into London, the paving of Chancery, Fetter, and Shoe Lanes, the ill-doings of the " London prentises," the state of the weather, the general health of the City, and the principal conflagrations. The destruction of monastic relics, and the gradual changes in religious worship, the names of those who were executed and burned, fill up this catalogue of interesting and curious events. When we remember that, in those days hanging, burning, boiling, and quartering were of almost daily occurrence, it will not appear strange that he should tell us the names of those who died in their beds. It is to be regretted, however, that many years are so curtly dismissed with merely a mention of the names of the Mayors. The

MS. closes with the year 1545; it is therefore not an improbable supposition that the writer died soon after that period. I cannot omit acknowledging myself indebted to that useful publication, "Notes and Queries," for some of the notes which will be found appended to this little Chronicle.

CLARENCE HOPPER.

London, Sept. 30 1858.

LONDON CHRONICLE

IN

THE TIMES OF KING HENRY THE SEVENTH AND KING HENRY THE EIGHTH.

[Brit. Mus. Cotton. MS. Vespasian A. xxv. f. 38—46.]

K. H. y[e] VII.

M. REMYNGTON, Mayir.[a] Then came yn my lady Kataryn, the Kyngges doughter of Castelle, in to Ingland.[b]

M. SCHAWE, Mayir.[c] Then was Prince Arthur, the son of K. H. the VIIth, maryid unto my lady Kataryn above sayd at Polles, and agaynst her commyng in to London was many goodly pageantes made in y[e] Citte at Alhalowtide when they weere maryed.

M. BARTILMEW REDE, Mayir.[d] Then dyid Prince Arthur[e] above sayd.

M. CAPELL, Mayir.[f] Then was London brydge a fyir.

M. WYNGGAR, Mayir.[g]

---

[a] Sir William Remington, A D. 1500.
[c] Sir John Shaw, 1501.
[e] In Easter week at Ludlow.
[g] Sir John Winger, 1504.

[b] 3rd October.
[d] Sir Bartholomew Read, 1502
[f] Sir William Capel, 1503.

M. Kneisworth, Mayir [a] Then came yn Dewke Phillip of Burgon agaynst his wille, w[t] tempast of wethir as he was goyng in to Spayn, whiche afterward was Kyng of Castelle.[b] Then was Polles wether cok bloun doun.

M. Haddon, Mayir.[c]

M. Browne and M. Elmar, Mayir.[d]

K. H. y[e] VIII.

M. Jenyngges, Mayir.[e] Then dyid K. H. the VIIth y[e] xxij day of Aprill. Then did y[e] deuke of Yorcke, whiche was brother unto prynce Artur afore sayd, mary w[t] my lady Kataryn, his brothur's wife, and was crounyd bothe kyng and quene on myd somer day sonday next after following.

M. Bradbery and M. Capell, Mayr͂s.[f] Then was Richard Emson and Edmond Dudley, which was afore chefe men w[t] Kyng H. the VII., behedid at Tour hille,[g] and then was Petté Waals in Temmys strete a fyir.

M. Kebyll, Mayir.[h]

M. Arsscheley, Mayir.[i]

[a] Sir Thomas Kneesworth, 1505.
[b] Driven by stress of weather into Plymouth on the night of the 15th January.
[c] Sir Richard Haddon, 1506.
[d] Sir William Browne, 1507, died during his year of office, and Sir Laurence Aylemer was chosen.
[e] Sir Stephen Jennings, 1508.
[f] Sir Thomas Bradbury, 1509, died during his mayoralty, and was succeeded by Sir W. Capel.
[g] 17th August.   [h] Sir Henry Keble, 1510.
[i] Sir Roger Acheley, 1511.

M. COPYNGER and M. HADDON, Mayr̃s.[a] Then went K. H. the VIIIth in to Fraunce w[t] a grete pouer; then y[e] Emprour y[t] then was whose name was Maximyanus and all his oste toke wages of ou[r] Kyng, and then was Torwyn[b] and Torney won and gevyn a way a none after. Then came yn Kyng Jamys of Skotland w[t] a grete powar full cowardly when ou[r] kyng was in Fraunce, and was kylde[c] for his labour. And on Saynt Laurans day was the Regent of Ingland and y[e] grete Caricke of Fraunce burnd,[d] whiche was ij the gretist shippes in Cristindom.

M. BROWN and M. TATE, Mayirs.[e]

M. MONOX, Mayir.[f]

M. BUTLAR, Mavir.[g]

M. REST, Mayir.[h] Then was the ill May day, y[e] Comous of the Citte and prentesis did rob and spoylle strayngars, and then was in dyverce places of the citte galons sett up and there was hanggid and quartarid: then was midsomer terme kepte at Oxford a litille while.

M. EXMEW, Mayir.[i]

[a] Sir William Copinger, 1512. He died during his mayoralty, and Sir William Haddon was chosen in his room.

[b] Therouenne in Picardy, won on the eve of St. Bartholomew.

[c] At Branstone near Berwick in the month of August.

[d] The great Carrick of Brest. With this vessel her captain Sir Piers Morgan and 900 men perished. In the Regent were drowned or burned her captain Sir Thomas Knevet, and Sir John Carew of Devonshire, with 700 men. See account of this engagement in Grafton's Chronicle.

[e] Sir William Browne, Sir John Tate, 1513.

[f] Sir George Monoux, 1514. [g] Sir William Butler, 1515.

[h] Sir John Rest, 1516. [i] Sir Thomas Exmewe, 1517.

M. Myrfyn, Mayr.[a]   Then was y[e] menoris[b] burnd.

M. Yarford, Mayir.[c]

M. Brigges, Mayir.[d]   Then was y[e] denke of Buckynggame behedid at Tour hill y[e] xvij day of Maye, Fryday, and is heryed at Freer Austens.

M. Mylburn, Mayr.[e]   Then came in the Emprou[r] Charlus whiche was son of y[e] Kyng of Castell afore sayd.[f]

M. Mundy, Mayir.[g]   Then came yn the Kyng of Denmark and his quene, and lay in y[e] Bisshop of Bathis place w[t] oute Tempull bar. And then was the Roodes[h] lost.

M. Bawdre, Mayir.[i]

M. Bayly, Mayir.[k]

M. Allen, Mayir.[l]

M. Seymer, Mayir.[m]

M. Spenser, Mayir.[n]   Then was no watche kepte at Midsomer.

M. Rudstone, Mayir.[o]

---

[a] Sir Thomas Mirfin, 1518.
[b] The Minories.
[c] Sir James Yarford, 1519.
[d] Sir John Bridges, 1520.
[e] Sir John Milborne, 1521.
[f] 26 May, at Dover.
[g] Sir John Mundy, 1522.
[h] Rhodes taken by Sultan Solyman, (eighth of the line of Ottoman,) on Christmas day.
[i] Sir Thomas Baldry, 1523.
[k] Sir William Bayley, 1524.
[l] Sir John Allen, 1525.
[m] Sir Thomas Seamer, 1526.
[n] Sir James Spencer, 1527.
[o] Sir John Rudstone, 1528.

MR. DODMORE, Mayir.[a] Then was y[e] Cardenalle pute oute of his Chauncelarship, and sir Thomas Moore, knyght, was made Chauncelar of Ingland.

M. PARGETAR, Mayir.[b]

M. LAMBART, Mayir.[c] Then came in a grete fisshe at Tynmouth.

M. PECOK, Mayir.[d] Then was quene Kataryn lady douagear put a side; then did the Kyng mary w[t] my lady An Bullen, and crounyd her queene at Westm' on Witsonday y[e] fyrst day of June.

M. ASKEW, Mayir.[e] Then was y[e] holy mayde of Kent,[f] ij freers, ij monkes,[g] and the parson of Aldermary[h] drawn from y[e] tour to Tiburn, there hanged and hedid.[i] Then was M. Doctor Taylar, prest, put oute of the Rolles, and M. Thomas Cromwell, temporalle man, made M. of y[e] Rolles and the kyngges secretary, and after that lord prevesele, and after that vicar generalle of alle Ingland and knyght of the Gartar, and after y[t] lord Chamburlayn and Erlle of Esex.

M. CHAMPNEY, Mayir.[j] Then was iij monckes of the Chartarhouse of London, and the Father of Syon, and a preest, drawen from the Towr to Tiburu, ther hangid, hedid, and quartarid; and after that iij monckes more of the Chartarhouse, and the Bisshop of Rochester,[k] behedid at Towr hille on Midsomer eve is eve, and is beryid in Barkyng churcheyard by the northe doore; and sir Thomas Moore, knyght, and Chauncelar of Ingland, beheded at Towr hille on

[a] Sir Ralph Dodmer, 1529.
[b] Sir Thomas Pargiter, 1530.
[c] Sir Nicholas Lambard, 1531.
[d] Sir Stephen Peacock, 1532.
[e] Sir Christopher Askew, 1533.
[f] Elizabeth Barton.
[g] Edward Bocking and Richard Dering.
[h] Henry Golde.
[i] 5th May.
[j] Sir John Champness, 1534.
[k] John Fisher.

saynte Thomas eve after mydsomer, and was beryid w*in the Tour
of London. Then the kyng made his owne hed to be pold, and
many lordes and knyghtes, and all the corte

M. ALLEN, Mayir.ᵃ Agayn twyis hole for him selfe. Then
dyid quene Kataryn a boute twelfe tide, and was beryed in Petur-
borow Abbey. The xvij day of May was behedid at Tour hille my
lord Rocheford, quene Ans brother, and M. Noris, M. Weston, M.
Breuton, and M. Marke,ᵇ for treson, and beryed alle in the Tour.
The xix day of Maye was behedid wᵗ in the Tour a pon a skaffold
queue An, and there was beryed. Then the kyng did mary wᵗ my
lady Jane Semer. Then dyid the kyngges bastard son denke of
Rechemondeᶜ at St. Jamys be yend Charyng ✠. Then roos up
the comous of Lyncolshereᵈ and of Yorke sheer. Then was dyverce
halidays put doune, and then began the abbes to go down.

M. WAREN, Mayir.ᵉ Then was my Lord Garet, the Erlles son
of Kildare in Erlond, and vᶠ of his unckulles drawen from the Tour
to Tiburn, there hanggid, hedid, and quartarid, yᵉ morow after
Candilmas day, Satterday. The xxv day of Maye, Fryday, Inⁱber

  ᵃ Sir John Allen, 1535.
  ᵇ *Read*, M. William Brierton, and M. Marke [Smeton].
  ᶜ Henry Fitzroy, Duke of Richmond and Somerset, natural son of King
Henry VIII. by Elizabeth, daughter of Sir John Blount, of Kynlet, co. Salop,
born 1519, married to the Lady Mary Howard, only daughter of the Duke of
Norfolk. He died on the 22nd of July, 1536, at the palace of St. James's, and
was buried at Thetford in Norfolk. His body was at the dissolution removed
to Framlingham, where there is a monument to his memory. His mother, who
possessed considerable personal attractions, was shortly after the birth of the
Duke of Richmond married to Gilbert Taylboys, son of Sir George Taylboys, of
Kyme, co. Lincoln. (See the Memoir of the Duke of Richmond, in the third
volume of Miscellanies published by the Camden Society, 1855.)
  ᵈ See Greyfriars Chronicle.   ᵉ Sir Ralph Waren, 1536.
  ᶠ The uncles of Thomas Lord Fitzgarret were Sir James Fitzgarret, Sir
John Fitzgarret, Sir Richard Fitzgarret, Sir Oliver Fitzgarret, Sir Walter
Fitzgarret.

day, was S[r] John Bowmer,[a] knight, drawn from the Tour to Tiburn, there hanggid and hedid, and his wife y[t] same our burnd in Smythfeld, both for treson; and Sir Stevyn Hamerton, knyght, and S[r] Nicolas Tempas [*knyght*][b], the Abbot of Fountans, the prior of Gisburgh, and Doctor Pekeryng, drawn from the Tour to Tiburn, there hanggid, hedid, and quartarid.   The ij day of June, Satterday, was S[r] Thomas Perci knyght, my Lord Lumley is son,[c] S[r] Frauncis Beygot, knyght, the Abot of Jarvis[d] [*and another moncke*], drawn from the Tou[r] to Tyburn, y[r] hanggid, hedid, and quartarid.   On Saynt Peturs eve was my lorde Hussey and Sir Robart Constabulle, knyght, and Mr. Aske, which was the hed Capten of alle, sent home in to the northe contre, and there they suffrid dethe; and M. Aske was hanggid in Yorke castelle [*upon y[e] walles*] in cheynys.   The last day of June, Satterday,[e] was my lorde Darcy, behedid at Tour hill.   On Saynte Edwardes eve, Fryday in the mornyng, was prince Edward boorn, the trew son of K. H. the VIII. and quene Jane his mothur, in Hamton Corte.   His godffathurs was the deuke of Norfock, and the denke of Suffocke, and the Bisschop of Caunterbery; and his godmothur was his owne sister, whiche was dooughter of quene Kataryn a fore sayd.   On saynte Crispyns eve, Wensday, dyid queue Jane in childbed, and is beryid in the castelle of Wynsor.

M. GRESSAM, Mayir.[f]   On saynt Mathies day th' apostulle the xxiiij day of February Sonday did the bisshop of Rochestere[g] preche at Polles cros, and had standyng a fore hym alle his sermon tyme the pictur of the Roode of grace in Kent that had byn many yeris in the Abbey of Boxley in Kent, and was gretely sought w[t] pilgryms, and

---

[a] Sir John Bulmer; the female here styled his wife was Margaret Cheyney, said to have been his mistress.

[b] The words within brackets printed in italics are erased in the original.

[c] George Lumley.

[d] Adam Sodbury.   The other monk (here erased) was the prior of Burlingtou, or Bridlington.

[e] The Greyfriars Chronicle places this on the 20th June.

[f] Sir Richard Gresham, 1537.   [g] John Hilsey.

when he had made an ende of his sermon the pictor was toorn alle to peces. Then was the pictor of saynte Savior that had stand in Barmsey Abbey many yeris in Southwarke takyn down. The xxij day of Maye, Wensday, was there set up in Smythfeld iij skaffoldes; the one was for my lord mayir and aldyrmen, and the denke of Norfock, the deuke of Suffocke, and my lorde prevesele; and the tothir for the bisshop of Worcetter, wheer on he stoode and preche; and the third skaffold was made over a gaynst ye bisshop, where on stode doctor Forrest, a graye freer of Grenewitche, whiche had byn many yers afore a grete precher at Polles crosse, and beside hym was there a pictor set up that was brought oute of Walis, that was callid Dervelle gadern,[a] and a litill beside that a payr of galous set up, and

---

[a] *Dervel Gadarn*, vulgarly called *Darvel Gatheren*, was son of Hywell ap Emyr Llydaw. He was the founder of Llanderfel church in Merioneth, and lived early in the 6th century. His festival occurs on the 5th of April. Michael Wodde (1554) thus alludes to him: "If the Welchman would have a purse he prayed to Darvel Gathorn." Lord Herbert of Cherbury, in his Life of King Henry VIII. mentions the destruction of this effigy. " A huge image called Darvel Gathorn being fetched out of Wales, served to burn Friar Forrest, condemned for counselling people in confession not to believe the King's supremacy, and to elude I know not what old blind prophesie."

The prophecy here alluded to was probably one which was current among the Welsh, viz., that this image would set a whole forest on fire, which prophecy was supposed to be fulfilled in the burning this friar. Upon the gallows to which he was attached these verses were inscribed:

> David Darvell Gatheren,
> As saith the Welshmen,
>   Fetched outlaws out of hell;
> Now he is come with spere and shilde,
> In harnes to burn in Smithfelde,
>   For in Wales he may not dwell.
> And Forest the frier,
> That obstinate lyer,
>   That wilfully shall be dead,
> In his contumacie,
> The Gospell doth deny,
>   The King to be Supreme Head.

when the Bisshop had made an end of his sermon, then was the freer had to the galous and hanggid a live by the myddylle and the armys w^t chaynys and there burnd, and the pictor cast in to the fyir to. Then was the pictor of our lady of Worcetter brought to London. Then was the Roode that stode in Saynt Margit Pattens churche yarde takyn a waye, whiche had stoud there xxxv yere and more, and with yn a litille while after there was burnd on a nyght over a gaynst the same churche a grete mayne of housis. Then was the pictor of ou^r lady of Walsynggame, whiche was the grettist pil- gremage in all Ingland, brought to London. Then was the Rood of Northor and Saynt Unckumber,^a that stode in Polles many yeris, takyn down, and ou^r lady of grace y^t had stond in Polles many yers.

The parson and parishioners offered a bribe of 40*l.* that this image should not be taken away. (See Ellis's Letters.)

^a Saint Uncumber is one of those saints whose names are not to be found in any calendar, and whose histories are only to be gleaned from the occasional allusions that we meet with in early writers.

Michael Wodde says, " If a wife were weary of her husband she offered oats at Powles, at London, to St. Uncumber."

> If ye cannot slepe but slumber,
> Geve otes unto Saynt Uncumber,
> And beanes in a certeu number,
> Unto Saynt Blaze and Saint Blythe.

Sir Thomas More, in his *Dialogue* (Book 2, chap. x.), makes special mention of Saint Uncumber, whose proper name it appears was Saint Wylgeforte. Speaking of the Saints, he says : " Some serve for the eye onely, and some for a sore breast. St. Germayn onely for chyldren, and yet will he not ones loke at them, but if the mother bryng with them a whyte lofe and a pot of good ale. And yet is he wyser than St. Wylgeforte, for she good soule is as they saye servyd and content with otys. Whereof I can not perceyve the reason, but yf it be bycause she shold provyde an horse for an evyll housbonde to ryde to the devyll upon, for that is the thynge that she is so sought for as they say. In so moch that the women hath therfore chaunged her name, and in stede of St. Wylgeforte call her St. Uncumber, bycause they reken that for a pecke of otys she wyll not fayle to *uncomber* theym of theyr housebondys."

It would seem also that there was a custom of offering of oats at " Poules," when a wife was weary of her husband, to St. Rhadegund.

Then was Saynt Thomas Schryne of Canterbery take down, whiche had byn many yeris a grete pilgremage. Then was every man, woman, and child, cõmaundid to lerne ther patar noster, ave and crede, in Englissche. Then hit was comaundid that no light should be set in churches a fore no Image, but alle take a waye.

M. FORMAN, Mayir.[a] Then was ye monckes of y[e] chartar house and alle y[e] freers in London put oute of ther housis. The ix day of Dissembar, monday, was beheddid at Tour hill the Erlle of Devensheer, othur wyis called Markes of Excetter, whiche was nye kyn unto the Kynge, and my Lorde Muntagewe and Sir Edward Nevelle knyght. The viij[b] day of Maye, Thursday, did alle the citte of London, every house holdar hym selfe and every servant y[t] he had y[t] was parsonabulle, had harnes les or more, and white cotes, and a red crose and a swerd set a pon the cote bothe be hynd and be fore, and all the chefe men had their cotes som of white satten and som of white damaske, and crossis and swerdes a pon them, as alle the tothir had. Then went they alle and my lord mayir and alle the Aldirmen to myle end w[t] owte Algate in the mornyng, and there they weere set forthe be five in a ray w[t] standardes born a fore them, and drounslates[c] playing a fore them alle the way, and they weer devidid in iiij battelles w[t] bowis, gonnys, mores-pikes, and billes, and so came thorow alle the citte and throw alle Westm', and aboute alle the newe parke, and came homward by saynt Jamys, and so over the feldes and thorow Holburn, and so home a gayn, and the Kynge stode at Westmynster over the new gate, and saw them alle from the begynnyng to the endyng. Then was no watche kepte at Midsomer. The ix day of July, wensday, was beheddid at Tour hille S[r] Andry Foskew[d] knyght and a knyght of y[e] Roodes.[e] Then did

---

[a] Sir William Forman, 1538.

[b] For account of this great muster see Grafton's Chronicle.

[c] Drounslate or dronslade, a kind of tabor or kettle-drum. (Vide H. Machyn's Diary.)

[d] Sir Adrian Fortescue.

[e] This knight of Rhodes was Sir Thomas Dingley.

the Bisship of Worcetter, whois name was Latemar, geve up his Bisshiprike unto the kyng.

M. HOLLYS, Mayir.[a]   The iij[d] day of Jenyver, Satterday, did the kyng and all y[e] noblis of y[e] Reme, and y[e] Mayir and all y[e] Aldirmen in ther best araye, and every craft in y[r] best a raye, went doun in ther barges to Grenwitche, and every barge as goodly drest as they coude device w[t] stremars and bannars, and ther the kyng did mete and reseve on Black heth my lady An, the Deukes doughter of Kleve, and made her queene of Ingland.   The xxviij day of July, wensday, was beheddid at Towr hille Thomas Crowmwelle, whiche that had byn a fore M. of the Rolles, and after that the Kynges secretary, and after that vicar generall, knyght of the gartar, Erlle of Essex, and lord Chamburlayn of Ingland; and my lord Hunggurford was beheddid ther that same tyme too.   The xxx daye of July, Fryday, was there drawn from the Tow[r] to Smythfeld vj doctors; iij of them was burnd, and the tother iij was hangged and quartarid; they y[t] were burnd ther namys were Docto[r] Barns, Docto[r] Garet parson of Honny Lane, Doctor Jherom vicar of Stepney; and ther namys that was quartarid, Docto[r] Powelle, Doctor Abelle, and Docto[r] Fethurstone; and the beddes of my lorde Croumwell and my Lorde Hungurford weer set up on London bridge, and ther bodyis beryid in the Towr.   This same yere was queue An the Deukes doughter of Kleve a fore sayd put a side.   The viij daye of August, sonday, did the Kyng mare w[t] my lady Kataryn Haward, the Dewke of Norfocke his brothurs doughter, and made her quene of Ingland. That yere dyid my lorde of Saynt Jhons in his bed, whois name was William Weston;[b] and that yere was new sargeantes of the queff[c] made and kepte ther Feste at Saynt Jhons; y[t] summer was a hoote and drye, and of grete dethe and greete of the agew.

[a] Sir William Hollis, 1539.

[b] Sir William Weston, Prior of St. John's, on the 5th of May, upon his hearing of the dissolution of his order.

[c] Coif.

M. Roche, Mayir.[a] That wynter was a very colde wynter, as was many yeris a fore. The xxvij day of May, Fryday, was the Countes of Salisbery beheddid w[t] in the Tow[r]. The xxviij day of June, Tewisday, was my Lord Lenard, Markes[b] behedid at Towr hill. The xxix day of June, Wensday, Saynt Peturs day, was my lorde Dakars of the Southe led be twene bothe the scherevis of London a fote from the Towr to Tiburn, and there was he hanggid. That yere the Kyng rode in progress to Yorke, and all the contre a boute. That yere was take doun y[e] loft in Polles, where yn stode y[e] Roode of Northor,[c] and Saynt Artnolles[d] schryne in Polles, and Saynt Edwardes schryne at Westm'. And the saide lorde Dakars a bove saide was beryid in Saynt Powlkurs churche, and y[e] said lord Dakars a bove saide was hanggid for robbre of y[e] Kyngges deer and murthur of y[e] Kepars.

M. Dormor, Mayir.[e] The x day of Dessember, Satterday, was M. Cowlpeppur, and M. Duran, drawn from the Towr to Tiburn. Cowlpeppur was heddid and Duran was hanggid and quartarid, both them for playing the harlottes w[t] with queen Kataryn that then was. The xiij day of Febreuary, Monday, was queene Kataryn and my lady Rocheford behedid, bothe in y[e] Towr of London. The xvij day of Marche, Fryday, was a mayde[f] boyld in Smythfeld, in a grete led,[g] for poysenyng of many y[t] she had doon. This yere came out of Erlond the Erll of Desmond, the great Aneelle,[h] and other grete lordes of Erlond, and did submyt them self to ou[r] Kyng: and this yere the Dewke of Norfocke, and other Erlles and lordes,

---

[a] Sir William Roche, 1540.

[b] Here the chronicler would appear to have made a slight ellipsis: Lord Lenard, Markes [Dorset's brother]. Lord Leonard Grey (son of Thomas 1st Marquess), created Viscount Graney, beheaded for high treason.

[c] Over this in the original is written in another hand *Northdore*.

[d] Probably St. Erkenwald's.   [e] Sir Michael Dormer, 1541.

[f] Margaret Davy.   [g] Leaden vat or caldron.

[h] O'Neil, created on that occasion Earl of Tyrone.

w[t] a grete army of men, [went] in to Scotland. This yere was Chauncere lane, and Fayter lane, and Scho lane, all thorow pavid; and this yere was the new chambers bildid in Tempulle garden; and alle this summer was a cold summer and wete

M. COTES, Mayir.[a] Then came in to Englond Kyng Jamys of Skotland, w[t] a pouar of men, after Alhalowtide, and one Johan a Musgrave, w[t] his company, met w[t] hym, and in that skyrmyssche y[e] Kyng was hurte or drounde, and there was takyn of y[e] Skottes xxj or xxiij presonars, that is to say, ij erlles, vj lordes, and alle y[e] othur knyghtis and jentilmen, and they were brought to y[e] Kyng to London y[e] xix day of Dessember. In the monthe of July the Kyng did mary w[t] my lady Kataryn Latemer, wedow, and made her queen. And this wynter was a colde wynter; hit began a fore Cristmas and lastid till Ester Monday, of and on, and of grete dethe, and parte of mighellmas terme was kepte at Saynt Albons; how be hit that M. Bowear was at that tyme Mayir, for the terme began after Alhalowtide, by cause of y[e] grete dethe y[t] was the summer be fore.

M. BOWEAR and M. WAREN, Mayr̃s.[b] This yere dyid in his bed at Crichurch, Sir John Audeley, lord Chauncelar of Inglond, and M. Bowear being Mayir. This yere was moche harm doon in Skotland, as Edynborow and othur townys burud and spoylid. And this yere the suffragis[c] that longgid to the lateny was songe in Englissche toung. And this yere y[e] Kyng, in the monthe of July,[d] went in to Fraunce w[t] a grete powar of men. And this yere was the yere of our lord God 1544, and the xxxvj yere of the Reng of Kyng Hary the viij; and this yere was Bullen[e] won and gevyn up. And this yere was the Angelle nobulle reysyd to viij s'.[f]

---

[a] Sir John Cotes, 1542.
[b] Sir William Bowyer, Sir Ralphe Warren, 1543.
[c] Prayers.   [d] 13th July.   [e] July 29th.
[f] By proclamation on the 16th of May. The first raising of the angel noble was in 1526. (Grafton's Chronicle.)

M. LAXTON, Mayir.[a] This yere was Jhūs stepulle, y^t stode in Polles churche yerde, take down, and no watche kepte at Midsomer, nor Midsomer terme kepte. The xxij day of August dyid in his bed in Gilford the Dewke of Suffocke, whois name was Charlus Brandon. The xij day of September, Satterday, in ye mornyng a boute five of the klocke, was Saynt Jylis churche burud, belles and alle, w^toute Crepille gate. The viij day of Octobar, Thursday, at nyght, aboute vij a klocke, was a ship of a nothur cuntre burnd at Blacke walle thorow mysse fortune of fyir.

M. BOWSS [Mayir].[b] This yere dyid my lorde Bawdwyn, chefe Justes of the comen place: then did my lorde Muntegew, whiche was chefe Justes of the Kyngges benche, make labor for to be chefe Justes of the comen place, and so he was. Then was my lorde chefe baarn of the Kyngges Excheker, whois name was Lister, made chefe Justes of ye Kyngges bench and sargeant, alle on oone day, the ix day off November, Monday, in the yere of ou^r Lorde God XV^cXLV, in the xxxvij yere of the Reng of K. H. the viij.

[a] Sir William Laxton, 1544.   [b] Sir Martin Bowes, 1545.

INDEX.

Abell, dr. hanged at Smithfield, 15
Acheley, sir Roger, mayor, 6
St. Alban's, 17
Aldermary, the parson of, hanged, 9
Aldgate, 14
Allen, sir John, mayor, 8, 10
Anne Boleyn, queen (*vide* Boleyn)
Anne of Cleves, qu. (*vide* Cleves)
Angel-noble, its value raised, 17
Arthur, the prince (son of Hen. VII.), marriage of, 5; his death, 6; remarriage of his widow, 6
Aske, mr. hanged in York Castle, 11
Askew, sir Christopher, mayor, 6
Audeley, sir John, his death, 17
Austin Friars, 8
Aylemer, sir Laurence, mayor, 5
Baldry, sir Thomas, mayor, 8
Baldwin, lord chief justice, his death, 18
Barking churchyard, 9
Barnes, dr. burned at Smithfield, 15
Barton, Elizabeth, the holy maid of Kent, executed at Tyburn, 9
Bath, bishop of, 8
Bayley, sir William, mayor, 8
Bermondsey Abbey, picture of St. Saviour taken down in, 12
Berwick, 7
Beygot, sir Francis, hanged at Tyburn, 11
Birlyngton, prior of, 11
Blackwall, a foreign vessel burned at, 18
St. Blaze, 13
Blount, sir J. 10
St. Blythe, 13
Bocking, Edward, hanged at Tyburn, 9

Boleyn, queen Anne, her marriage and coronation, 9; beheaded and buried, 10
Boulogne taken, 17
Bowes, sir Martin, mayor, 18
Bowyer, sir William, mayor, 17
Boxley Abbey, the picture of the Roode of Grace belonging to, destroyed, 11
Bradbury, sir Thomas, mayor, 6
Brandon, Charles, Duke of Suffolk, his death, 18
Branstone, King James of Scotland killed at, 7
Brest, 7
Bridges, sir John, mayor, 8
Brierton, William, beheaded at Tower Hill, 10
Browne, sir William, mayor, 6, 7
Buckingham, duke of, beheaded, 8; his burial, 8
Bulmer, sir John, hanged at Tyburn, 11; his lady burned at Smithfield, 11
Burgundy, duke of, driven ashore at Plymouth, 6
Butler, sir William, mayor, 7
Canterbury, archbishop of, 11
———— shrine of St. Thomas of, taken down, 14
Capell, sir William, mayor, 5, 6
Carew, sir John, 7
Carrick, a vessel called "the Great Carrick of Brest" destroyed, 7
Castile, 5; king of, 6, 8
Champness, sir John, mayor, 9
Chancery lane, paving of, 16
Charing Cross, 10
Charles V., the emperor, arrival of, 8
Charter House, three monkes of, hanged, 9; monks of expelled, 14
Cheyney, Margaret, burned in Smithfield, 11

Christchurch, 17
City, grand muster of the,
———— pageants, 5
———— riots, 7
Cleves, queen Anne of, her a and reception, 15; divorc
Constable, sir Robert, execu
Copinger, sir William, may
Cotes, sir John, mayor, 17
Cripplegate, 18
Cromwell, Thomas lord, h pointments, made Ea Essex, 9; beheaded at Hill, 15
Culpepper, mr. beheaded,
Dacres, lord, hanged at T 16
Darcy, lord, beheaded at Hill, 11
Davy, Margaret, boiled at S field for poisoning, 16
Denmark, the king of, with his queen, 8
Dering, Richard, hanged, 9
Dervel Gadarn, destruction Welsh image so called, at S field, 12
Desmond, earl of, arrives Ireland, 16
Devonshire, earl of, *alias* Ma of Exeter, beheaded at Hill, 14
Dingley, sir Thomas, behea Tower Hill, 14
Dodmer, sir Ralph, mayor,
Dormer, sir Michael, mayor
Dorset, Marquess of, 16
Dover, 8
Drounslates, a kind of tabor 14
Dudley, Edmund, behead Tower Hill, 6
Duran, mr. hanged at Tybu
Edinburgh, 17

Edward VI., birth of, and names of his sponsors, 11
St. Edward, his shrine at Westminster taken down, 16
St. Erkenwald's shrine in St. Paul's removed, 16
Essex, earl of, Thomas Cromwell made, 9; decapitated, 15
Exeter, Marquess of (*vide* Earl of Devonshire)
Exmewe, sir Thomas, mayor, 7
Fetherstone, dr. hanged at Smithfield, 15
Fetter lane paved, 16
Fisher, John, bishop of Rochester, executed, 9
Fitzgarret family, execution of, 10
Fitzroy, Henry (illegitimate son of King Henry VIII.), his decease, 10
Forrest, dr. (a grey friar of Greenwich), burned at Smithfield, 12, 13
Forman, sir William, mayor, 14
Fortescue, sir Adrian, beheaded at Tower Hill, 14
Fountains, abbot of, hanged at Tyburn, 11
France, Hen. VIII. goes into 7, 17
Garet, dr. (parson of Honey Lane,) burned at Smithfield, 15
Garet, lord, 10
St. Giles's Church, (Cripplegate,) entirely destroyed by fire, 18
Gisburgh, the prior of, hanged at Tyburn, 11
Golde, Henry, hanged at Tyburn, 9
Graney, viscount, 16
Greenwich, 12, 15
Gresham, sir Richard, mayor, 11
Grey, lord Leonard, beheaded at Tower Hill, 16
Guilford, 18
Haddon, sir Richard, mayor, 6, 7
Hamerton, sir Stephen, hanged at Tyburn, 11
Hampton Court, 11
Henry VII., 5; death of, 6
Henry VIII. marries his brother's widow Katherine, 6; goes into France, 7; divorces queen Katherine and marries Ann

Boleyn, 9; causes his head and those of his court to be polled, 10; marries lady Jane Seymour, 10; death of his illegitimate son, 10; birth of his son prince Edward, and death of queen Jane, 11; reviews the great city muster from the new gate at Westminster, 14; goes by water with the mayor and aldermen to Greenwich and receives on Blackheath Ann of Cleves, 15; divorces Ann of Cleves and espouses Katherine Howard, 15; rides in progress to York, 16; causes the queen Katherine to he beheaded, 16; marries Katherine Latimer, 17; goes with a great retinue into France, 17
Hilsey, John, (bishop of Rochester), 11
Holborn, 14
Hollis, sir William, mayor, 15
Honey Lane, 15
Howard, lady Mary, 10
———— queen Katherine, marriage of, 15; beheaded, 16
Hungerford, lord, beheaded at Tower Hill, 15
Hussey, lord, executed, 11
Hywell ap Emyr Llydaw, 12
St. James's, 10, 14
James IV. of Scotland makes a treacherous inroad during the absence of the king of England, and is killed, 7
James V. of Scotland comes with an army into England, and in the skirmish is killed or drowned, 17
Jane (queen Jane Seymour), *vide* Seymour
Jarvis, abbot of, hanged at Tyburn, 11
Jennings, sir Stephen, mayor, 6
Jerome, dr., (vicar of Stepney,) burned at Smithfield, 15
Jesus steeple in St. Paul's taken down, 17
St. John's, 15
———— lord of, dies, 15
Ireland, 10, 16

Katherine of Arragon rival in England, 5; to Prince Arthur, 5; to king Henry VIII. and ed queen, 6; her deat her daughter, 11
———— (Howard) quee Howard)
———— Latimer, marria Henry VIII, 17
Keble, sir Henry, mayor,
Kent, the Rood of Grace stroyed, 11
———— holy maid of (*vide*
Kildare, 10
Kneesworth, sir Thomas,
Knevet, sir Thomas, 7
Kyme, 10
Kynlet, 10
Lambard, sir Nicholas, m
Latimer, Hugh, (bishop c cester,) resigns his see,
———— Katherine, marr king Henry VIII. 17
Laxton, sir William, may
Lights before images in c prohibited, 14
Lincoln, 10
Lincolnshire riots, 10
Lister, (lord chief baron exchequer,) made chief of the king's bench, 18
Litany, prayers sung in 17
Llanderfel church, 12
London, 13, 17; friars pelled, 14; sheriffs of,
London Bridge, conflagra 5; heads of the lords well and Hungerford on, 15
Ludlow, 5
Lumley, lord, 11
———— George, hanged burn, 11
St. Margaret Patten, chu of, its rood taken away
Maximyanus, the emperor milian I.), 7
Merioneth, 12
Midsummer watch, 8, 14
Milborne, sir John, mayor
Mile-end, great city muste
Minories, the, burned, 8

INDEX.

Mirfin, sir Thomas, mayor, 8
Morgan, sir Piers, 7
Monoux, sir George, mayor, 7
Montague, lord, 14
——— lord chief justice of the king's bench, made chief justice of the common pleas, 18
More, sir Thomas, made lord chancellor, 9; beheaded at Tower Hill, 9
Mundy, sir John, mayor, 8
a'Musgrave, John, his encounter with king James V. of Scotland, 17
Neville, sir Edward, 14
Norfolk, duke of, 10,11,12, 15,16
Norris, mr., beheaded at Tower Hill, 10
Northor, the rood of, taken down from St. Paul's, 13; removal of the rood loft of, 16
O'Neil, the great, with other lords, comes out of Ireland, 16
Oxford, 7
Paternosters and other prayers ordained to be in English, 14
St. Paul's, 5; weathercock blown down, 6; roods taken away, 13; rood loft and shrines taken down, 16; Jesus steeple removed, 17
St. Paul's cross, preaching at, 11
Pargiter, sir Thomas, mayor, 9
Peacock, sir Stephen, mayor, 9
Percy, sir Thomas, hanged at Tyburn, 11
Petty Wales, conflagration of, 6
Philip, duke of Burgundy, driven by stress of weather into England, 6
Pickering, doctor, hanged at Tyburn, 11
Plymouth, 6
Powell, doctor, hanged at Smithfield, 15

Read, sir Bartholomew, mayor, 5
Regent, the, a great vessel so named, burned, 7
Remington, sir William, mayor, 5
Rest, sir John, mayor, 7
St. Rhadegund, 13
Rhodes, taken, 8
——— knight of, beheaded, 14
Richmond, duke of (vide Fitzroy)
Roche, sir William, mayor, 15
Rocheford, lady, beheaded, 16
Rochester, bishop of (John Fisher), beheaded, 9
——— (John Hilsey), preaches at St. Paul's cross, 11
Rudstone, sir John, mayor, 8
Salisbury, countess of, beheaded in the Tower, 16
Salop, 10
St. Saviour, picture of, 12
Scotch prisoners taken, 17
Scotland, 7, 16, 17
Seamer, sir Thomas, mayor, 8
St. Sepulchre's church, 16
Seymour, lady Jane, marriage of, 10; birth of her son and her death, 11
Shaw, sir John, mayor, 5
Shoe Lane, paving of, 16
Smeton, Mark, beheaded at Tower Hill, 10
Smithfield, 11, 12, 15, 16
Sodbury, Adam, 11
Solyman, sultan, 8
Somerset, duke of, (see Fitzroy) 10
Southwark, 12
Spencer, sir James, mayor, 8
Stepney, vicar of, 15
Suffolk, duke of, 11, 17
Talboys, Gilbert, 10
——— sir George, 10
Tate, sir John, mayor, 7

Taylor, dr. 9
Tempest, sir Nicholas, han Tyburn, 11
Temple Bar, 8
Temple Garden, new cha built in, 16
Thames street, 6
Therouenne taken, 7
Thetford, 10
Thomas of Canterbury, sai shrine taken down, 14
Tournay taken, 7
Tower Hill, 6, 8, 9, 10, 14
Tower of London, 9, 10, 16
Turwyn taken, 7
Tyburn, 9, 10, 11, 16
Tynemouth, 9
Tyrone, earl of, 16
St. Uncumber, 13
Wales, 12
Walsingham, picture of o of, 13
Warren, sir Ralph, mayor,
Welsh prophesy, 12
Westminster, 14, 16
Weston, mr. beheaded at Hill, 10
——— sir William, prio John's, his death, 15
Windsor Castle, burial of Jane at, 11
Winger, sir John, mayor,
Wolsey, cardinal, displace the chancellorship, 9
Worcester, picture of our I 13
——— bishop of (Hu timer), 12, 13, 15
St. Wylgefort, 13
Yarford, sir James, mayor,
York, 16
York Castle, 11
York, duke of, 6
Yorkshire riots, 10

Lightning Source UK Ltd.
Milton Keynes UK